# BROKEN BUT NOT FORGOTTEN

**MINISTER DOROTHY WATKINS**

# Chapter One

## He Left ….

The Word speaks of an inheritance left for the children's children. My daddy, Mr. Lee Willie Holmes, left just that.

I so vividly remember him preparing us for the winter. Everyone has witnessed ants in a line, hauling food to the ant bed, we've heard of bears going into hibernation, birds flying south, but no one prepared us like my daddy. I can smell it now, pine needles boiling, the scent filling the house like a candle. Even corn shucks were put to a boil to be drank as a hot tea, all to prepare my sisters and brothers and I for the winter. It wasn't the drink of choice, but it was just what we needed to get us from winter to spring. He would make sure that we ate healthy. We had a garden every garden season. We were all excited!  He would pick the baby peas, he loved to eat the uncooked baby peas, and corn. He said eating raw vegetables would make us healthy. I can remember we were even raised to eat a whole onion at a time with salt. We ate whatever he ate, and it was so delicious. I even think about the times when my mom would fry chicken, my dad would eat the marrow off the bone. He told us that was the way to eat the inside of the bone, and to this day some of my sisters and brothers still eat their chicken that way.

My daddy was a man of his word. If he said he was going to do something, that's what he did.  I can recall every time he said he was going to kill a rabbit, he killed a rabbit! One day we were riding down the road and daddy begin shooting out of the window! He had seen a rabbit, and you better believe we brought it home with us. I loved to smell that rabbit cooking. But I was just a daddy's girl. I loved his presence.

My daddy instilled in me at a young age, that I could be and do whatever I wanted to. I can remember it like yesterday my daddy, wearing a blue work uniform, good hair, nice looking light skinned man. I can still hear him, as I'm sitting on his lap, "you can do anything!"

I remember when I was about 10 years old my dad gave me my first driving lesson. I was so excited. My daddy said, "Take the wheel, press the gas, and drive!" I was so excited and nervous at the same time, but I knew my dad was right there by my side. I didn't have anything to worry about. My mom, sisters, and brothers were in the car and my mom would say, "Slow down, you driving too fast!" My dad would laugh. But I didn't have any fear because he was right there.

I think my daddy always told me I could do and be anything because he could do anything. I remember when I was ten years old and my dad did the most amazing thing! He was a mechanic as well as he worked a full time job. This one particular time my daddy fixed a motor by using the skin fat of a hog to make it run. It was one of the coolest things ever! We rode for a while until it finally quit. I guess I could say he got oil in our blood, because my three sons are also mechanics.

I believed with all my heart that I could do anything because daddy could. I believed it until he left us. When daddy left my dreams left. I had no reason to dream. I had no reason to want to be anything. I had no reason to reach because he wasn't there to see me do it. My daddy didn't die, or he wasn't dead, but I died inside. Oh how I loved him. I wasn't the only child but I had a bond with my father. He was my protector, my friend, my motivator. But he was gone. I can't explain how my other 9 sisters and brothers felt, but I was a lost child.

I don't hate my mom and dad for getting a divorce. I just wish they could have had the skills to reach out to someone that could've helped them and also to help us, the children. We didn't know how to cope, because I was alone in a home of many. We had good parents, but they were no longer good for each other and it bled on us. The decision was made, but we all lost. Nobody won. He left.

## Chapter Two

## SHATTERED

I was a child but I had experienced enough hurt at a young age to last me a lifetime. I couldn't deal with this. I needed a safe place to escape and still be present. I didn't have grandparents around, the way I'm around for my grandchildren. Most days, I was present physically, but emotionally I had locked myself in a shell. I had become like a turtle, sticking my head out here and there. But when things hurt, got hard, didn't feel right, I'd just go back into my shell. I didn't have anyone to talk to in a house full of sisters and brothers. I wondered if they were feeling what I was feeling, because I was lost. I didn't want to be found unless it was daddy that found me.

I would walk out on the porch looking up that long driveway looking for his car. I was hoping that he was coming to see me. There were days that I walked down that long driveway to catch the bus for school, I wondered what my day would be like. I was very shy, and felt very uncomfortable around others. I couldn't look people straight in their eyes.  There were times I felt so broken. I wanted to go in the bathroom and hide  sometime I thought people could see how broken I was and a try to hide  I Loved  school I always wanted to make good grade in school I love the school, but it was hard. Sometimes after my dad left the thing that made it so easy it was. I had some nice teachers. I don't know if they had seen my pain or not, but I know when They seem like they cared about me and always gave me a smile it made my day I often wondered on the school bus if he would be home when we got there. I would write poems about it.

My dad's leaving left me shattered like glass. I wondered if momma cared I wondered did anyone care because I was helpless. One night after feeling at my lowest, I was passing by my mom's bedroom and overheard her praying. I couldn't believe what I was hearing! My mother knew how to pray. I just froze, I couldn't move, I was inspired and I was just in amazement. I had never seen nor heard my mom pray. Now, even as an adult, I credit my still being here to the prayer I heard that night. When I think about my sisters and brothers, when I talk with them and when we embrace each other, all the credit goes to the prayer I heard my mom pray on that night. Even though my heart was shattered, it was my mom's prayer that lifted me that night. As I think about it this year 2025, I realized that God heard my mother's prayer. She saved me in that moment, because in that moment I saw love, peace, vulnerability, concern, reverence, trust, faith and a mom that really loved her family.  Even though my heart and my dreams were shattered, GOD gave me a silver lining.  There was hope, I wanted to pray just like my momma. Seeing her down on her knees, I saw humbleness, I was so used to seeing her strong.

I had a STRONG desire to be validated and recognized by my dad. Even when he had left home, I imagined my dad walking me down the aisle when I got married. I wanted him to tell me he approved of the man I would be date or marry.

Every time, I got my report card, I imagined my dad coming home and me meeting him at the door with my report card and he would say, "Good job my girl!"

Some of you may have experienced rejection and disappointment from divorce the way I have, or maybe a lack of love in the home, church hurt, betrayal and many other things. Sometimes these things cause us to have low self-esteem, a feeling of wanting to belong, wanted to be accepted and loved. Rejection will come in this life, but we must forgive and let it go.

My daddy still didn't come back home! Even after all this time had passed and my mom's good prayer had went up that night. But my momma was still taking care of us. It was just something about my daddy though, whenever I would see my daddy, my heart would just light up. He would give me money, but I wouldn't spend it. I would just hold on to it, all because he gave it to me. Daddies are just as important to girls as boys, or even more, because I really felt that I couldn't make it without him.

## Chapter Three

## "DISASTER MET DISASTER"

My cousin's friend introduced me to his friend, and when I saw him, he had a big afro. His hair was very long, he was a very nice looking young man. He was very respectful, very polite and he was just as shy as I was. My mom liked him and I did too. I had my mom's approval and later I got my daddy's approval that's all I needed.

Later, he asked me to marry him. We were so in love, and we had each other' back. We felt that LOVE was all we needed to survive. At least that's what we thought, until one day we found ourselves facing some decisions that had to be made. We didn't know what to do. I felt in my mind that if my dad had been around he would know what to do. I valued my dad's opinion so much. I knew he would have the answer, and if he didn't have the answer, he would tell me everything would be okay.  This is when I realized my pain was still there and burning deep.

As time went on, we had six wonderful children while we fought against our own past dealings with anger, hurt, low self-esteem, anxiety, and depression. We realized that we weren't much help to our children, because we were broken. We were trying to raise children when were so incomplete. We were trying to raise children and, we ourselves couldn't even express how we felt about anything. How could we tell them to speak up, to express themselves, to love themselves? I was locked in a shell and my husband had his own shell. We were like to brick walls facing each other.

My husband began to share with me about his life. Things that I didn't know about him, that he never told anyone. He had kept it locked inside, where no one could hurt him again. He shared with me about being in school and being told that he would never be anything, he was told that he wouldn't graduate. I had noticed that he felt insecure about a lot of things that he did, like fixing the lawnmower, He would say, "You think I can't fix it" And I asked him, "Why do you always asked me that?" His reply was, "That's what I always been told, "I can't!" I realized that just as he felt no one believed in him, I always felt that no one heard me. I would always repeat whatever I was saying, and my husband would bring it to my attention that I had already said that once. Even now, I still try not to repeat myself. But I wanted him to know that I have some hang-ups as well. He didn't talk about it much, but when he did, I listened. My husband was all that I had. I trusted him like my daddy. I looked to him as my father figure. I looked for my daddy in him. I looked for him to be my peace, protection, and my everything, but he was suffering like I was. He was lost like I was. My hurt and his hurt came together at that time, we were an explosion waiting to happen. Neither of us knew what to do. We were both dealing with trauma from our past. We did the only thing that we knew to do, and that was too stay in our own world away from other people. We tried to guard our hearts the best way we knew how.

    We chose to walk in the light of God. We chose God and we kept crying out to him, "Why God Why?" We were fighting to survive. We were facing so many challenges in our lives that we knew it had to be God, because we could have easily made some bad moves and ended the marriage. But we chose to WIN! We chose to fight the good fight of faith and stand! 1 Timothy 6:12. We could have easily said that this is too much for us! But we chose not to quit. When I think back over my life, my husband and I have been through so much together. But together we agreed to let some people go, negative talk was hurting us. We decided that we would not allow anyone to be negative to us anymore. It was hurting our marriage, negativity would bring even a good marriage down so we chose not to deal with it. People that didn't want us together we didn't entertain them. Rejection after rejection from here and there, we chose not to deal with it. We had each other and we had God. We fought with faith and we are still winning!

    We didn't have much but we had love for each other. I remember when he would walk through the door from work with a half a piece of candy bar in his hand. He ate half and left me the other half. I thought that was one of the sweetest thing I had ever experienced. We both worked, so we both would come home and cook together. We would always clean together. He always made the bed. I never had to make the bed, I always said to myself, "God has his hand on our life." God has a plan for us.

Jeremiah 29:11; for I know the plans that I have for you and Romans 8:31; if God is for you who can be against you?

## Chapter Four

## LOVE LIFTED ME

In most movies or in most stories when the Calvary comes everything is all over with, but not in our case. God sent LOVE for me and my family. When we thought nothing else could help it was Love that came our way. Our prayers were not in vain, praise God!!! We had prayed and held on and help showed up! Hallelujah! God sent the Calvary for me and my family

My husband, I and the kids ended up moving back in with my mom while we searched for a house. We lived in a little community called Horse Nation, a place I will never forget. Just thinking about how much the people in this little community meant to us warms my heart.

It was there, in Horse Nation, where my life begin to change. We discovered a church down the road within walking distance, if we wanted to walk. My mom, sisters and brothers had been attending this church for about four months before we started to attend. Seeing this church brought back memories of my childhood. I thought about when my brother and I went to church with our grandmother and aunt we attended church service every Sunday. The people were very nice. I was glad to get back in church. Then, three months later, I got my very first job. I was so excited. When I got to the workplace, I saw some of the same people I had seen at church and some were even my neighbors. As I now look back at my life, I would say God had a plan for me. He put me right in the middle of the people that he would use to help me. Thank You Jesus!

There was a lady name, Mrs. Mae Clarett, she came over to welcome me, and she was the lead person on the job. I also met Mrs. Willie Jean Clarett's sister, Mae. One day Mae invited me to attend a home Bible class. My husband and I both went to that Bible class that night, and it was a night that we would never forget! Our lives were changed. We dedicated our lives back to the Lord and we were filled with the Holy Spirit. It was so amazing to be in that meeting and feel the presence of God. Some of the people from work were at that house meeting too. One day I needed a ride home and I ended up riding home with Mrs. Mae and Willie Jean. They didn't stay far from where I lived, so my husband would pick me up when he got off work. But every day before we got home, Mrs. Mae and Willie Jean would stop at the Hwy. 389 Store. It was just the snack we needed before we got home. As I smile to myself, we would eat liver cheese, lunch meat and crackers every day, and it was so good. I didn't have money all the time to buy me a snack. But I never had to worry, because if one ate the other one ate.

Then, instead of going home, I started spending more time with them when I got off work. Even when my husband got off work, he started to spend more time at their house as well. We became more like family than co-workers. They became my spiritual moms. Mrs. Mae was a mom that would tell you about God and then she would sing to you about what she just told you. There were so many days she would cook salmon for me and my husband, it would be so good. We all ate together. I can't help but laugh, this is when I started drinking coffee. We would drink so much coffee! Mrs. Mae's husband was so precious to me and my husband. I don't know if he knows that he meant so much to us.

We always had a laugh when my husband would get Mr. Clarett to work on his truck. He would always say, "Ain't nothing wrong with that truck!" We would laugh, but I thought the same thing, there was nothing wrong with that truck.

Mrs. Willie Jean was that mother that would tell you what she expected of you. She taught me so many life skills that I couldn't possibly name them all. So many nuggets she gave me in every conversation. She taught me to treat people with kindness and love. And whenever you make a mistake, keep going. She told me to always keep God first in my life. This lady, even taught me how to handle business. She went through the process of showing us how to buy our first home. One thing I will never forget that she preached to us, have life insurance, house insurance, and car insurance. And to this very day, if I have nothing else, l have insurance.

She was an amazing cook! And when she cooked, it was a sight to see! She cooked more than two things, unlike me. I never cooked more than two things for supper. We enjoyed eating from her table many days. On Saturdays, we would go to her house and eat breakfast with the family.

Mrs. Willie's husband, Mr. Palmer, became my spiritual dad. I remember so clearly that he always had a garden, and when went to visit him, he would always give me two big cabbages. He would be so happy to do that for me. I don't think he knew how happy it made me because I love cabbages.

Their children became my sisters and brother. Mrs. Willie called me Dot and she would say, "You are the oldest and I expect more out of you." What could I say? I was twenty-two years old at that time and I had so much respect for whatever she said. But being called her daughter, I thanked God! Just to hear that made me feel like a daughter. She just doesn't know what that meant to me, how she shaped and molded my life. I remember the time she sewed me clothes to wear on special days at work. She made sure that we had food to eat at home and then she would bring me a sandwich to eat at lunch. Sometimes, I felt so unworthy to have someone in my life that cared so much for me.

Her entire family treated us like their family. It was just so amazing to me that when we moved into our first house, she and her whole family and my co-workers and my aunts all gave us a house warming. Whenever I was sick, they came and cleaned my house, not one person, but all of them. They were a family that stayed together no matter what. I gained a whole family that didn't just tell me about love, they show me what love looked like.

My own mother and my two spiritual mothers have played such a significant role in shaping me. Their love and guidance has guided me throughout my life. Lord knows that I owe so much of who I am to their influence. I deeply appreciate them for the incredible impact they've had on me. It brings tears to my eyes and rejoicing to my heart every time I think about my life. I will always put God first, because that's how I will always win. They all taught me this and I pray that it will continue through generations to come.

Along with my spiritual mothers their children, families, their friends, and so many others to name have had an alarming impact on my life and became my family.

I have two special aunts, Wilma and Shawn Holmes and so many others, I just can't call the names that has such an impact on my life at the workplace and still do. We are all like glue, and we are all sticking together. I feel so good that I am stuck with them. So many times I felt like I didn't deserve to have someone that cared so much for me and my husband, but now I still see God was in the plan and He still is today.

God sending this cavalry into my life at one of my lowest times, displayed His love for me through them. It was love that lifted me when I couldn't do for myself.

# Chapter Five

## Forgiveness

There was a time when my life felt completely overwhelmed by stress. I was constantly battling different illnesses. I was so tired. I had been through some difficult times. I had low self-esteem, and the weight of life challenges were resting on me. I was just bogged down. One day I cried out to God because I was so tired of the way things were in my life. And the Lord spoke to me clearly. The Lord said, that before my body could be healed, I needed to forgive and release. I realized then that the hurts and pains that I had been through were holding me back. I knew that the word of God said to forgive others so that you shall be forgiven; Matthew 6:14-15. I went before God and forgave those people that wronged me and I forgave myself for holding onto anger and bitterness.

Forgiveness, changed me. I never could have imagined that forgiveness would feel so good. I felt like a new person. But there was this one person that I hated. I never knew what hate felt like until this person did my husband and I wrong so many times. My dislike for this person soon just turned into hate. I also learned to that God is something else, because He will put us to the test. Because it was about a week after I had forgiven everyone in my life, I saw that person. It was amazing to me that I was so free until I wanted to run and hug them. That day, I told myself I would never hate another person. It didn't feel good to hate someone.

As a child or God, I knew I had the right to go before God and receive my healing or whatever I needed. According to Hebrews 4:16 says, "let us therefore come boldly unto the throne of grace," so I knew that I could go before Him now with confidence and with that fear that He would hear my prayer. I thank God that my husband and I underwent a transformation, we were changed by forgiving and leaving the past behind, because we both needed to forgive some people. And because we forgave, the word of God renewed our minds. We begin to read and meditate on the word of God, and found out that we didn't have to carry the burdens of this life. We learned to just cast it all to Jesus. We found out that God loves us with a perfect love that is everlasting. A Love that He delights in His children, and wants us to have an eternal relationship with Him.

2 Corinthian 6:18 God called us His sons and daughters. I was and I'm still so excited to have a Heavenly Father that loves me so much. There was so many times I felt like God had abandoned me. The truth is he never left my side. He was there all the time. I didn't have to fear or worry, the Lord always gave me strength. Deuteronomy 31:8, says, "He would never leave me nor forsake me."

Psalm 18:33 says, "He made my feet like the feet of a deer and set me on high place. I cast all my cares on the Lord, for I know He cares for me. When I took my hands off my situation that's when God did something about it. I chose to walk in the abundant life that God had for me. I began to let the Holy Spirit lead and guide me in the right path. I realized when I am walking through the valley, I don't have to fear.

One thing I realize is that there will be rejection in life, we just have to know how to handle it. Let go and forgive. John 10:10 talks about a thief that comes to kill, and destroy because his goal is to disrupt and harm people lives. He comes to steal our joy, peace, and relationship with God. He doesn't want marriages to work. He wants to destroy the whole family, but Jesus wants to give life and have it more abundantly. I refuse to live my life in bondage again Now that I know he came to heal my broken heart.

Just because I was born again and filled with the Holy Spirit and in church didn't make me free. I had to forgive and walk in love every day. My husband and I chose to forgive and pray to clean our hearts every day from unforgiveness, bitterness and whatever we could think of and ask God to fill us with his love.

I chose to forgive not only for myself, but for my children, grandchildren, and the generations that are coming behind me. It's not all about me. It's about my seed having things broken off their lives. I refuse to allow it to be passed down to my children and their children. The pains and hurt that I dealt with, I don't want them to have to deal with that, being stuck, and not free, not knowing how to get out of bondage. I want to show them what total freedom looks like in the Lord. I want to show them how they can take the word of God and break things off their life, and to declare and decree things in their life the same way I do in my life.

# Chapter Six

# I Found My Voice

Life is a journey. Life is a process that undergoes many stages. After my dad had left us, my life was shattered. I went into a shell and married a man that was in a shell. Our children grew up in a space where no one expressed themselves. We were all trapped until love found us. The Lord spoke and the word forgiveness, unlocked the door for us. It didn't just unlock the door for us, but it also unlocked my voice. I found my voice! I thought that I would never find my voice again. It was trapped deep down inside my body screaming for help, and wondering could anyone hear my silent cry. As I look back over my life, God never left me. He was there all the time. When I was home with my dad and even more after my dad left, God didn't leave. But he sent someone to help me, a husband that love me so much that even in my mess, he was right there in the mess with me. Then the Lord sent a family that pointed me to God! I found out that I had a Heavenly Father, and develop a relationship with Him. I talked to Him. I loved on Him and I'm in love with Him. In the presence of God is where I found my joy and my peace.

I have such confidence in my Heavenly Father, that when He tells me something I can trust Him. The word says He's a Man that He cannot lie, I can run to my Father. He is someone I can trust more than anyone else. I can't think about what if my dad hadn't left what my life would have been like? Who knows because I was pointed in the right direction? I found a Heavenly Father that means so much to me. He demonstrated his love on the cross and He did it through other people. I know one thing, my voice was lost but now it's found!

I refuse to be silent again. I will fight for what is mine. I will not be put in a shell again. I will tell everyone about the goodness of God, I know who I am. I am a warrior! I have news for the devil, "You came to steal and destroy, but I have a voice that I will shout to the world, there's a Man that came to set the whole world free nobody has to stay in bondage!" Hallelujah!

I will praise Him! I will worship Him! I know now that God inhabits our praise, so I will praise Him at home! I will praise him in the worship place! GLORY!! Nobody knows my story like I do! In the presence of God I find my answer, because we communicate, we talk to each other.

God has a plan for my life. Was this the plan that he had for me? I don't know, but all I know is that I am not going down. I am pulling others out of the pit. I refuse to let my loved ones be left behind. I walk the floor and do warfare for them. That is where I find myself early in the morning, doing warring for someone else and my family. The devil cannot have them!

I could have sat around and thought that my life was so messed up and couldn't be fixed, because I came from a broken home. But I don't have time to look back at the past. I look forward to the future that God has for me. I know too much about God and His plan for my life, and the works that He called me to do. There are so many people that are hurting, and looking for answers. There are people that need to be pulled out of darkness, they feel that no one loves them, no one cares for them and thinking that God has forgotten them.

Finding my voice, I can now say, I do not blame my mom and dad for the things that transpired in their marriage any they had to end it. Now I realize it could have been me that had to have a divorce, but God. He didn't leave me. That's why I shout for joy! Thank God, who the Son sets free is free indeed. I was broken but not forgotten.

# CHAPTER 7

## He Left for the Last Time

This time when my dad left, I was prepared for his leaving. The Lord had begun to deal with me about 10 years earlier. One day I got the call that he wanted to go to the hospital. I had felt it in my spirit that there would be a home going for someone close to me. I told my brother about it that morning and he said he had felt the same thing. When we arrived at my dad's apartment we called 911. They came and took him to the hospital. We got there before everyone and waited on the doctor in the ER. We just talked and had so much fun just out of nowhere. My dad said he did not have enough life insurance, but we assured him that it was okay, we had him covered. Daddy said he wanted to live at least five more years. We told him that the Lord was able. But in my heart, I knew he was not coming home. Because the Lord had showed me, and had prepared me for my dad's home going.

Dad started saying that he was feeling better and he wanted to go home. The doctor said they would keep him overnight and observe him for the next three days. My sisters, brothers, nieces, and grandchildren were coming and going we had so much fun. It was joy, like a reunion. We all were happy to see our dad back in our lives, and then on top of that, he had built relationships with some of the grandchildren. It was so beautiful. Then on the third day, everything turned. My dad had a stroke. He was hanging on. He knew he was here and he would try to talk to us. In my heart, I didn't want him to leave. There were many days that I would tell him that I loved him. When we lived at home,  he wouldn't never say he loved me back. Then this one day he said I love you too. I knew he loved me. He just didn't know how to say it. But after that every time I told him I loved him he would say it back. I told him about 10 times a day and every time he responded back I love you too.

   I stood there watching my dad leave me for the last time. This time we didn't lose. We all gained. I gained this time! This time I was able to bring comfort to my dad by telling him God loved him, and making sure his heart was prepared for heaven. Everything that was taken from me as a little girl, it couldn't be taken any more. I had found my place in God! I knew who I was. I knew my earthly father was about to leave me again, but my Heavenly Father would never leave me. The Lord talked to me and showed me things to come like he did about my father. John 14: 26 says, the Holy Spirit is a comforter. I thank the Lord for being my Comforter every day. My dad was in the hospital for one month, and every day I made sure he knew that we loved him and God loved him. I told him continually that everything was going to be okay.

My dad always said when the Lord comes back, he would be ready to go. That's always been his words and now he wants to stay. He was lying there looking at his family, standing there looking at him. He had another chance to be with his family but now he was getting ready to leave them again. There were so many words spoken over him from his family. Everyone told daddy that they loved him and his response was he loved them too. His leaving this time I believe brought healing to the family. I believe in my heart if he had a chance to do it again, he would've done things differently, because now he wanted to give love. I can still remember him whispering the words," I love you." And I in response would whisper back to him, "I love you too."

Every time I wanted to break down and cry and I did cry, I remembered the words of God that said He will give me peace that surpasses all understanding. I took the peace of God and walked in it. I wasn't going to let nothing take my peace again. As I walked in the peace of God I was able to stand in the church and be the Mistress of Ceremony at my daddy's home going service. I was so proud and happy to give him a home going because I knew it was well with the Lord. The day my dad went home to be with the Lord, I went into his room and I said dad this is the end. And I believe that I heard the Spirit of the Lord say, "It's only the beginning." I believe it was the beginning for my family to hear the words coming from my dad that he loved them and them saying it back to him. I believe the Lord always brings opportunities around, but what we do with them is our choice.

As I end this book, I've learned so much on my journey. We often see others glory, but we don't know their true story. As I begin to heal, I begin to educate myself as well. Even after healing sometimes we still can see scars, every now and then we still feel the wounds as they may get bumped every now and then, or we may become triggered. But what I've listed see different types of wounds.

Understanding emotional wounds.

1 The father wound

2 The mother wound

3 Church hurt

4 Rejection

These are only a few. Emotional wounds can have a profound effect on an individual's mental health and relationships. Each of these wounds can shape a person's sense of self their interactions with others and their spiritual journey.

Forgive:

If you forgive others that trespassed you, your Heavenly Father will also forgive you, but if you do not forgive other that trespassed, neither will your Father forgive you of your trespasses. Matthew 6:14-15.

PRAYER:

Heavenly Father I come before you today to forgive_____for the hurt they have caused me just as you have forgiven me. I choose to forgive them, release me from bitterness and anger I hold and, help me to move forward with peace in my heart, in the name of Jesus. Amen

**When you begin a relationship with God, you don't just become God's friend you become His child. God delights in you and wants the best for you. He wants to fill**

your life with joy and blessings. So this is how God loves the world. He gave his one and only son so that everyone who believes in Him would not perish, but have everlasting life John 3:16

Hebrew 13:5, I will never leave you non-forsake you.

Speak, sing declare who God is and His power, praise and worship can break down walls and shackles

Praise can refresh our spirit and invite God presence. When we praise we are strengthened.

We can speak decree and declare over our life.

I declare that I am strong and courageous Isaiah 54: 17.

**I declare that I will run and not grow weary Isaiah 40 31**

**I declare that God loves me unconditionally as he love his son.**

**Freedom**

Thank God for freedom, when you invite God's power into your pain, you can experience freedom. If you are struggling and need help, you can seek help from a counselor or therapist are a spiritual leader.

www.ingramcontent.com/pod-product-compliance
Lightning Source LLC
LaVergne TN
LVHW012131070526
838202LV00056B/5951